MW00737984

TENNIS TALK
PSYCH YOURSELF IN
TO WIN !!!

Books by Paula Whittam

THE WILL TO WIN !
Affirmations to Help You Know and Get What You Want!

TENNIS TALK, PSYCH YOURSELF IN TO WIN !
Affirmations for Mental Fitness in Tennis.

TENNIS TALK
PSYCH YOURSELF IN
TO WIN !!!

Affirmations for Mental Fitness in Tennis

Paula Whittam

Sapphire Publishing Corporation (Bahamas)

Revised Edition, second printing 1996

Published simultaneously for the USA, Canada and the UK

First published in 1994, revised edition printed 1995 and 1996

by *Sapphire Publishing Corporation (Bahamas)*
Charlotte House, Charlotte Street, PO Box N-341, Bahamas

Correspondence:
Sapphire Publishing Corporation (Bahamas)
BP 55, 06240 Beausoleil, France
or
PO Box 88, Lytham St.Annes, FY8 1ZN Lancashire, England

Edited by Laura F. Windsor

Printed by Gilliland Printing Inc., Kansas, USA

British Library Cataloguing in Publication Data
A catalogue record for this book is available from the British Library

ISBN 976-8148-04-7 paperback

DEDICATION

To my parents
Who taught me how to never give up

To my brothers, Neil and Ian
Who taught me how to go out there and win

ACKNOWLEDGEMENTS

A big thank you to my friends and everyone who gave me a helping hand along the way.

Many thanks to Jennifer Linett for all her support and assistance on legal matters in the USA and to Denys Laurence for his help on legal matters in Europe.

A very big thank you to Gilly Collinson, Joseph Galliano, Christian Watine, Gaelyn Larrick and Bram Larrick for their advice, support and professionalism.

Last but not least, many thanks to Nicky Fraser for reviewing and proof-reading the text.

CONTENTS
****

PREFACE

Alongside the physical training and preparation before playing your tennis matches, comes MENTAL FITNESS.

This book is a useful tool to incorporate into your overall preparation, so that these affirmations become a natural and instinctive part of your mental make-up. It is also ideal reading material, if you have to wait more than a few minutes to play your match, to give yourself your own positive PEP-TALK.

Believing in yourself is PARAMOUNT in all levels of play. So why not take your game up a level, if not more, by building on that potential?

INTRODUCTION

To win is what all of us set out to achieve in our tennis game but how many times have we let a match slip away because of lack of concentration, wandering thoughts, negative chatter in the back of our minds or simply because of doubts in our own ability?

I have written this book as I know affirmations are a powerful tool, acting as a mental trampoline always assisting us to bounce back in times of stress. These affirmations will help you focus and maintain your concentration, quieten that negative chatter and eliminate those thoughts which gradually erode your self-confidence and create self-doubts. In short, they will help you find that winning spirit which lives within you.

Affirmations are positive statements we can use to put supportive and empowering suggestions into the conscious mind. Repetition of affirmations starts to move these positive thoughts from the conscious to the subconscious mind.

The conscious mind observes, thinks and evaluates. Whereas, the subconscious mind does not observe, think or evaluate, it merely carries out the orders (the thoughts) it receives from the conscious mind and **works to bring those thoughts about as reality.**

Thoughts in our conscious minds come from outside influences and conditioning: parents, friends, television, radio, books, society and culture etc. These thoughts move from our conscious to our subconscious minds in two ways, by repetition or through emotion about the thoughts.

In the past you may have put negative thoughts into your subconscious mind. For example, by often telling yourself you cannot do something you limit yourself. **Since your subconscious mind is non-judgemental, it accepts whatever is impressed upon it or what you consciously believe.**

It responds accordingly, working 24 hours a day to bring about the "fruit" of your habitual thinking.

Open up your mind and break through the limitations you have placed on yourself. The only limits are those you have set for yourself. Start to use your subconscious mind to achieve your goals and realise your potential.

Affirmations become a natural and instinctive part of your mental make-up the more you read, write or listen to them. Use only those affirmations you feel are right for you, better still, form your own personal affirmations. Relax and quieten your mind before proceeding, as your mind will be more receptive to accepting your affirmations in this state.

Do repeat your affirmations often, a good time to do this is just before sleeping or just as you wake since your mind is in a deeply relaxed state. Try recording them on a cassette to make it easier and add background music. Choose your favourite music, something stimulating to be motivated and psyched or quieter music for when you relax or sleep. Use music to evoke your emotions as this gives a double impact, to assist your affirmations to move from your conscious to your subconscious mind, through both emotion and repetition.

Also, do work through the Negative Clearing Exercise at the end of each section since it is important to clear any negative thoughts out of your mind to avoid them interfering with your affirmations, by neutralizing the positives or creating conflict of thought.

Read and refer back to this book regularly, carry it with you so you can give yourself a positive pep-talk whenever needed. Above all, be relaxed, flexible and enjoy yourself!

Paula Whittam

Section 1

SELF-MOTIVATION

Setting the goals you want to achieve
and knowing why.

Maintaining direction, energy
and enthusiasm towards them.

SELF-MOTIVATION

I have the ability to win this match
... I believe in myself.

I have the ability to win this match
... I believe in myself.

I have the ability to win this match
... I believe in myself.

SELF-MOTIVATION

I have the strength, power and energy to win.

I have the strength, power and energy to win.

I have the strength, power and energy to win.

SELF-MOTIVATION

*I have the determination and resiliance
to achieve my goals.*

*I have the determination and resiliance
to achieve my goals.*

*I have the determination and resiliance
to achieve my goals.*

SELF-MOTIVATION

— Your practical pointer :

After each winning point,
I show a positive physical reaction.

After each winning point,
I show a positive physical reaction.

After each winning point,
I show a positive physical reaction.

NOW IT'S YOUR TURN
SET YOUR OWN GOALS RELATING TO SELF-MOTIVATION :

MY GOALS	WHAT I WANT	WHY
Number 1		
Number 2		
Number 3		

Create your own affirmations and pointers below (always in the present tense). Find out what's right for you because this section is not complete without *your* input.

Self-Motivation is the ability to maintain direction, energy and enthusiasm towards your personal goals and ambitions and is part of your creative potential. Energy and enthusiasm come from joy, fun and loving what you are doing and are vital elements in enabling you to release your creativity and remain motivated and fulfilled.

It is also important to know exactly what you want, otherwise how can you achieve it? Define your goals precisely and know why you wish to achieve them as this assists you to know yourself and develop a personal awareness. Put your goals down on paper, for example:

Goals
1.   Improve my mental fitness
2.   Improve the consistency of my serve
3.   Improve my ranking

Why
1.   To help me win more matches
2.   To assure I win my service game
3.   For my self-satisfaction

To be self-motivated it is important to believe in yourself and be committed to your goals otherwise you will lower your energy levels and the possibility of achieving what you want. Develop and maintain an inner enthusiasm and drive to assist you to have constancy of purpose and prevent loss of direction towards your goals. Everyone needs encouragement and support from their family, friends or coach but do not depend on it as without your own drive, your motivation will be greatly diminished and probably short lived. Find a balance between both your inner drive and outer support.

Notice what enhances your motivation to help you maintain high energy levels and to keep going even in the event of set-backs. Do not push yourself too hard in order to avoid "burn-out" and remain relaxed and flexible. Sometimes we do not achieve what we want simply because we are trying too hard. Above all, enjoy what you are doing, as this gives you yet more energy.

Now form you own personal affirmations to go with your goals, always in the present tense, avoiding "I will" and "I want", keeping the format simple, for example:

1.   I say no to all negative thoughts and fill my mind with positives
2.   I am relaxed and serve consistently
3.   I always play to the best of my ability

You may find when you start saying these affirmations to yourself or outloud that you immediately counter them with a negative thought. Do the following exercise to help clear any negatives and ensure your thoughts are a constant source of positive energy. Repeat it systematically after each topic since affirmations are effective as long as you do not immediately counter them with a negative thought, otherwise they will be neutralized and ineffective.

NEGATIVE CLEARING EXERCISE

Write each negative thought down as it occurs to you, on a blank piece of paper, **which you can rip up and throw away later.** Think about them for a while and work out which ones have the most power over you. Counteract each one by writing your own positive affirmation(s) or by using an affirmation from the preceding section.

Examples of possible negative thoughts:

1.   I tense up in competition and then I don't play well
2.   I get cross when I start making double faults
3.   This is stupid, how can I improve my ranking using my thoughts?

Affirmations to counter the negatives:

1.   I am relaxed and ready to play well
2.   I am calm and serve consistently
3.   I think positively and my mental fitness increases every day

Repeat this process, clearing and releasing each destructive thought as and when it arises, replacing it with something positive. Then feel and visualize yourself as vividly as possible in the context of your new affirmation.

Section 2

SELF-CONFIDENCE

Believing in yourself and feeling you play well.

Knowing you can achieve your goals.

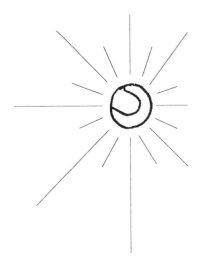

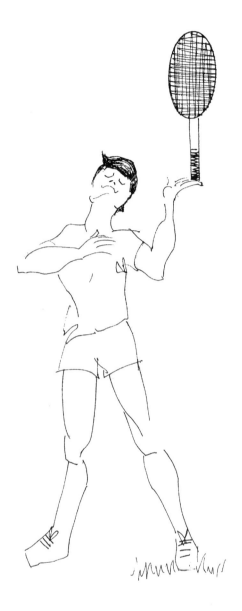

SELF-CONFIDENCE

I know I can win
    ... I believe in myself.

        I know I can win
            ... I believe in myself.

            I know I can win
                ... I believe in myself.

SELF-CONFIDENCE

I have strength and stamina ...
     the power is within me.

I have strength and stamina ...
     the power is within me.

I have strength and stamina ...
     the power is within me.

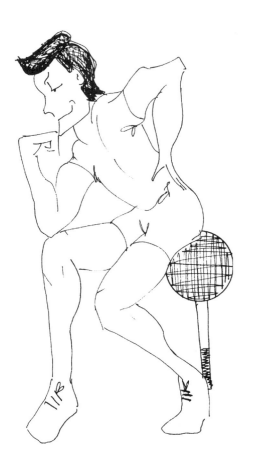

SELF-CONFIDENCE

*I have the mental and physical ability
to win this match.*

*I have the mental and physical ability
to win this match.*

*I have the mental and physical ability
to win this match.*

SELF-CONFIDENCE

— Your practical pointer :

*I NEVER show my opponent what I'm thinking
or feeling when I'm unhappy.*

*I NEVER show my opponent what I'm thinking
or feeling when I'm unhappy.*

*I NEVER show my opponent what I'm thinking
or feeling when I'm unhappy.*

NOW IT 'S YOUR TURN
SET YOUR OWN GOALS RELATING TO SELF-CONFIDENCE :

MY GOALS	WHAT I WANT	WHY
Number 1		
Number 2		
Number 3		

Create your own affirmations and pointers below (always in the present tense). Find out what's right for you because this section is not complete without *your* input.

Self-Confidence is believing in yourself and your ability to play well, knowing you can achieve your goals. It is the basic foundation for anything you want to achieve.

To build your self-confidence, be aware of your feelings and how you react in certain situations, in other words, know yourself. Recognize if you play best when in a calm, relaxed state or if you need to be "pepped-up" with adrenalin running. For many players the ideal combination is a mixture of the two, being "ready to go" yet calm and quiet. Serenity is a noticeable element of positive energy. Ask yourself questions, how are you feeling on court and off court, do you feel well prepared for your match, have you given yourself optimum conditions? Recognize fear and anxiety before matches and deal with them. Affirmations coupled with deep breathing and relaxation can be one effective way to assist you in overcoming pre-match nerves. Visualize yourself playing well and winning, remember, action follows thoughts.

Affirmations help build your self-confidence and form a cushion of positive thoughts that will immediately be available for you in moments of stress and pressure. Repeat your affirmations regularly: in training, whilst getting ready for a match, warming-up prior to a match, changing ends in matches, early morning when you wake and last thing at night before sleeping. Doing so will start to impregnate your conscious mind with positive thoughts which will move into your subconscious mind and in turn become second nature to you and automatic in your reactions. Form your personal affirmations to go with your objectives, for example:

Goals
1. Minimise match nerves
2. To be physically relaxed in matches
3. To believe in my ability

Affirmations
1. I am relaxed and calm, I'm doing okay
2. My arm is relaxed and I hit my shots well
3. I can handle anything that comes my way

Make your goals and affirmations relevant to your tennis/life and especially when starting out, make them attainable. As you progress, think in expanded and unlimited ways but be realistic and practical when applying them to your individual situation.

Having confidence is not just a question of believing in yourself but knowing you can achieve whatever you set out to do. This is why affirmations are so powerful because they will assist you to know you can achieve whatever you set out to do, **when you continue using them on a regular basis.**

Use the following exercise to clear any negative thoughts you may have related to confidence, so that your thoughts are a constant source of positive energy.

NEGATIVE CLEARING EXERCISE

Write each negative thought down as it occurs to you, on a blank piece of paper, **which you can rip up and throw away later.** Think about them for a while and work out which ones have the most power over you. Counteract each one by writing your own positive affirmation(s) or by using an affirmation from the preceding section.

Examples of possible negative thoughts:

1.   I'm frightened I won't play well and will lose badly
2.   I am tense and stiff, so I won't play well
3.   What if I make a fool of myself?

Affirmations to counter the negatives:

1.   I always play to the best of my ability
2.   I am relaxed, calm and confident
3.   I believe in myself and I know I'll be okay

Repeat this process, clearing and releasing each destructive thought as and when it arises, replacing it with something positive. Then feel and visualize yourself as vividly as possible in the context of your new affirmation.

Section 3

SELF-DISCIPLINE

Maintaining your momentum
by planning what to do and how.

Putting your plans into action
and modifying them when needed.

SELF-DISCIPLINE

I remain calm and relaxed all match
... I believe in myself.

I remain calm and relaxed all match
... I believe in myself.

I remain calm and relaxed all match
... I believe in myself.

SELF-DISCIPLINE

I always play to the best of my ability.

I always play to the best of my ability.

I always play to the best of my ability.

SELF-DISCIPLINE

I act clearly and decisively
... I let nothing upset me.

I act clearly and decisively
... I let nothing upset me.

I act clearly and decisively
... I let nothing upset me.

SELF-DISCIPLINE

— Your practical pointer :

I preserve my physical energy
... as much as possible.

I preserve my physical energy
... as much as possible.

I preserve my physical energy
... as much as possible.

NOW IT 'S YOUR TURN
SET YOUR OWN GOALS RELATING TO SELF-DISCIPLINE :

MY GOALS	WHAT I WANT	WHY
Number 1		
Number 2		
Number 3		

Create your own affirmations and pointers below (always in the present tense). Find out what's right for you because this section is not complete without *your* input.

Self-Discipline means maintaining your momentum by planning what to do and how to do it, putting your plans into action and modifying them when needed. It is having the determination and perseverance to follow through and apply yourself to achieving your goals.

After each topic is a section to define what you want to achieve in relation to motivation, confidence, discipline, esteem, improvement and concentration and focus. For example under motivation, you may wish to improve your mental fitness. Here you will need to define what in relation to self-discipline will assist you attaining mental fitness (or whatever goals you have noted down). Do this for each topic, for example:

Goals/Action

1. *Motivation* Improve my mental fitness
   Discipline Cut out all negative thoughts if I miss a shot
2. *Motivation* Improve the consistency of my serve
   Discipline Hit 100 practice serves a week
3. *Motivation* Improve my ranking
   Discipline Complete each work section in this book

1. *Confidence* Minimise match nerves
   Discipline Learn meditation and self-hypnosis
2. *Confidence* Be physically relaxed in matches
   Discipline Practise deep breathing and relaxation
3. *Confidence* Believe in my ability
   Discipline Repeat my affirmations regularly

Form any affirmations, if you feel they are appropriate but essentially this section is for mapping out "action needed" to help you attain your goals.

Work towards performing your best at all times by developing your self-discipline. This involves many facets such as controlling your emotions, choosing how you react in situations, eliminating negative thinking in order to achieve your full potential and reducing pressure, since the only person who puts pressure on you is YOU. Quality and consistency of play depend on how you think and how you feel emotionally.

Keep a rational balance, knowing that performance levels vary but that regular use of your affirmations will assist you to play to the best of your ability. Remember to give yourself optimum conditions when saying, listening or writing out your affirmations. Just saying them "any old way" is not likely to do much good, remember to be relaxed and in a receptive state. Intelligent use of affirmations will release much power. Repeating your affirmations in a meaningful way, understanding what you are saying and why, will assist your mind to believe and accept what you state as true. Affirm with ease, never co-ercing your mind to accept what you are saying, otherwise you will set up energy blocks.

You may find it easier to record your affirmations onto a cassette and listen to them regularly, especially whilst and before sleeping, as you wake or on a journey. If you record your affirmations, consider using some background music, preferably your favourite music or something which evokes emotion in you. This will give a double impact of both emotion and repetition to help your affirmations move from your conscious to your subconscious mind. Remember, thoughts move from the conscious to the subconscious mind through either emotion about the thought or by repetition. Think about using different types of music for different times, quiet music for relaxing or sleeping and stimulating music to help you be motivated and psyched.

Again, do the following exercise if you feel it is required:

NEGATIVE CLEARING EXERCISE

Write each negative thought down as it occurs to you, on a blank piece of paper, **which you can rip up and throw away later.** Think about them for a while and work out which ones have the most power over you. Counteract each one by writing your own positive affirmation(s) or by using an affirmation from the preceding section.

Repeat this process, clearing and releasing each destructive thought as and when it arises, replacing it with something positive. Then feel and visualize yourself as vividly as possible in the context of your new affirmation.

Section 4

SELF-ESTEEM

Nurturing, encouraging and
treating yourself well.

Feeling positive about yourself
both on and off court.

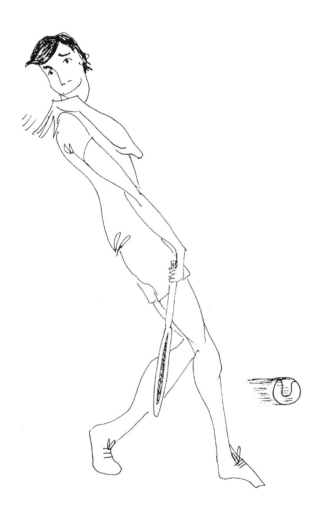

SELF-ESTEEM

Whatever the outcome, I am kind to myself
... I believe in myself.

Whatever the outcome, I am kind to myself
... I believe in myself.

Whatever the outcome, I am kind to myself
... I believe in myself.

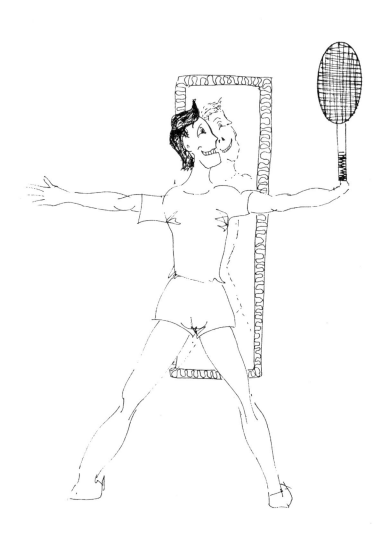

SELF-ESTEEM

*I praise and encourage myself
when I play well.*

*I praise and encourage myself
when I play well.*

*I praise and encourage myself
when I play well.*

SELF-ESTEEM

I forgive myself if I make a mistake
... I forget it and get on with the game.

I forgive myself if I make a mistake
... I forget it and get on with the game.

I forgive myself if I make a mistake
... I forget it and get on with the game.

SELF-ESTEEM

— Your practical pointer :

I keep my posture straight and
     my head UP at all times.

I keep my posture straight and
     my head UP at all times.

I keep my posture straight and
     my head UP at all times.

NOW IT'S YOUR TURN
SET YOUR OWN GOALS RELATING TO SELF-ESTEEM :

MY GOALS	WHAT I WANT	WHY
Number 1		
Number 2		
Number 3		

Create your own affirmations and pointers below (always in the present tense). Find out what's right for you because this section is not complete without *your* input.

Self-Esteem means nurturing, encouraging and treating yourself well, feeling positive about yourself both on and off court. It means taking care of your needs, respecting your feelings, loving and understanding yourself.

Know how to treat yourself when you lose a match. Do not judge such a loss in relation to your value as a person as it will lower your self-worth and create negative feelings which in turn will affect your confidence. This is counter-productive and to be avoided at all costs.

Examine why you have lost a match and use it as a learning exercise but do not destroy your self-confidence because of it. It is essential to be able to differentiate between how you play a match and your overall value as a person. When you devalue yourself as a person it will affect you in practice, in competition and even in life. Use errors as a mini-alarm, that signal you need to look at something, but do not over-analyse. Learn from your errors and mistakes, turn the negatives into positives and grow from them, improving your game and your attitude towards yourself.

Form your personal affirmations for self-esteem to team up with your main objectives, for example:

Goals
1.   Not to be hard on myself if I miss a shot
2.   To be aware of how I am feeling on court
3.   Know how to react if I lose a match

Affirmations
1.   I forgive myself if I make a mistake
2.   I listen to my feelings and respect them
3.   Whatever the outcome I am kind to myself

As well as saying your affirmations to yourself or recording them, you may like to write them out each day. Pick two or three of your own affirmations and write them out 10-20 times, once a day, for two weeks.

Feel each word and see what you are writing about in your mind's eye. Quieten your mind, focus and concentrate on what you desire. Imagine the end result and keep your mind centred on it. Whatever your conscious mind believes your subconscious mind accepts and acts upon.

Remember it has taken time for you to form any negative blocks you may have (over the years of growing up, learning and being conditioned) so be patient whilst you "de-programme". It need not take the same length of time to "de-programme" that it took for you to form the blocks but do be patient and follow through.

Clearing any negatives may make you go through a period of self-examination but persevere and get them out of your system.

NEGATIVE CLEARING EXERCISE

Write each negative thought down as it occurs to you, on a blank piece of paper, **which you can rip up and throw away later.** Think about them for a while and work out which ones have the most power over you. Counteract each one by writing your own positive affirmation(s) or by using an affirmation from the preceding section.

Examples of possible negative thoughts:

1. You idiot, you don't play well!
2. I can't believe you fluffed that sitter!
3. What kind of tennis do you call that, useless!

Affirmations to counter the negatives:

1. I believe in myself and my ability to play well
2. I forgive myself if I make a mistake, I forget it and get on with the game
3. I always do the best I possibly can

Repeat this process, clearing and releasing each destructive thought as and when it arises, replacing it with something positive. Then feel and visualize yourself as vividly as possible in the context of your new affirmation.

Section 5

SELF-IMPROVEMENT

Progressing steadily and attaining your goals.

Knowing continuous improvement is necessary.

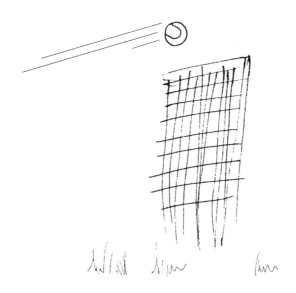

SELF-IMPROVEMENT

I always keep my goals in sight
*   ... I believe in myself.*

I always keep my goals in sight
*   ... I believe in myself.*

I always keep my goals in sight
*   ... I believe in myself.*

SELF-IMPROVEMENT

I have the wisdom and patience necessary,
to achieve all my desires.

I have the wisdom and patience necessary,
to achieve all my desires.

I have the wisdom and patience necessary,
to achieve all my desires.

SELF-IMPROVEMENT

*I recognize my progress and
I continue onwards and upwards.*

*I recognize my progress and
I continue onwards and upwards.*

*I recognize my progress and
I continue onwards and upwards.*

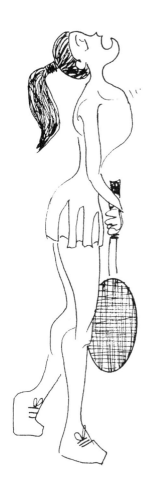

SELF-IMPROVEMENT

— Your practical pointer :

I breathe DEEPLY and
    exhale slowly between every point.

I breathe DEEPLY and
    exhale slowly between every point.

I breathe DEEPLY and
    exhale slowly between every point.

NOW IT'S YOUR TURN
SET YOUR OWN GOALS RELATING TO SELF-IMPROVEMENT :

MY GOALS	WHAT I WANT	WHY
Number 1		
Number 2		
Number 3		

Create your own affirmations and pointers below (always in the present tense). Find out what's right for you because this section is not complete without *your* input.

Self-Improvement is progressing steadily, understanding how to improve to achieve your goals and knowing that continuous improvement is necessary. It is having honesty in self-evaluation, flexibility and the intent to improve.

Along with goal setting and personal planning, it is important to review and modify your plans as and when needed. At the same time monitor your progress at regular intervals, using a diary or personal note book. Develop the ability to be able to look at yourself positively but with accuracy, recognizing any areas where further progress is desirable and plan how to achieve this.

If you feel there has been insufficient progress in a particular area, examine why. If a goal is proving harder than you imagined to attain perhaps you need to re-assess the situation. How easy or difficult do you **believe** it is to achieve? Are you unknowingly creating a block or need to change your perception of the situation? Look at your ability to change your belief and how much you really want to achieve your goal. The extent you wish to do something has a profound effect on your belief that you are able to achieve it and will also affect how determined you are to succeed.

Watch over your thoughts both on and off court and avoid thoughts which neutralize your affirmations or create conflict in your mind. Conflict of thought is when you feel and think phrases like "I'll never succeed", "This is hopeless" and "I can't win". Avoid such phrases since your subconscious mind always accepts the dominant idea. For example, it is no use saying to yourself "I have the strength, power and energy to win this match" if in the same breath you are thinking "I can't win, my opponent is a better player than me", as your subonscious mind accepts what you feel to be true. Remember your subconscious mind merely executes the orders (your thoughts) which come from your conscious mind through repetition or emotion and works to bring them about as circumstances for you.

Review your main goals and work out any modifications, then form any new affirmations, if needed. For example:

Goals

Motivation	**Improvement**
Improve my mental fitness	Stop all negative back chat
Confidence	
Minimise match nerves	Keep my emotions at bay
Esteem	
Know how to react if I lose	Learn from my matches

Affirmations for Improvement

1. I STOP all negative thoughts
2. I remain calm and centred
3. I learn from all situations

Be aware if an affirmation is kicking up a negative reaction each time you say or hear it. In this case you may find it beneficial to make your affirmation more impersonal so that you do not generate conflict. For example, if when saying to yourself "I remain calm and centred" you are thinking and feeling "No I'm not, I'm scared stiff", you may find it more appropriate to say "My self-control is increasing every day". Alternatively use repetition of individual words such as:

Relax, relax, relax   or combinations like:

Calm down/breathe deeply/relax

Complete the following exercise also, if needed.

NEGATIVE CLEARING EXERCISE

Write each negative thought down as it occurs to you, on a blank piece of paper, **which you can rip up and throw away later.** Think about them for a while and work out which ones have the most power over you. Counteract each one by writing your own positive affirmation(s) or by using an affirmation from the preceding section.

Repeat this process, clearing and releasing each destructive thought as and when it arises, replacing it with something positive. Then feel and visualize yourself as vividly as possible in the context of your new affirmation.

Section 6

CONCENTRATION AND FOCUS

Directing all your attention, thoughts and energy towards the right thing at the right time.

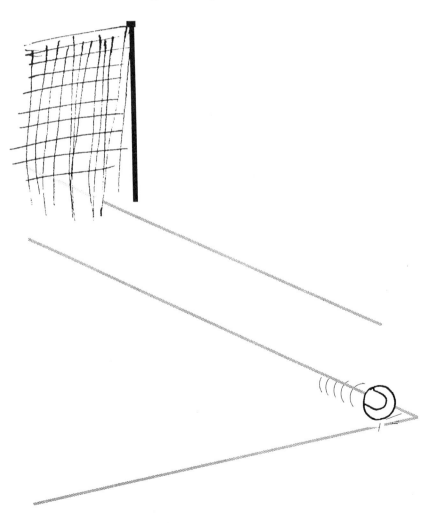

CONCENTRATION AND FOCUS

I remain lucid ...
I give my complete attention during each point.

I remain lucid ...
I give my complete attention during each point.

I remain lucid ...
I give my complete attention during each point.

CONCENTRATION AND FOCUS

*I have the ability to concentrate
and focus all my energies.*

*I have the ability to concentrate
and focus all my energies.*

*I have the ability to concentrate
and focus all my energies.*

CONCENTRATION AND FOCUS

I forget all other points and
focus on the one at hand.

I forget all other points and
focus on the one at hand.

I forget all other points and
focus on the one at hand.

CONCENTRATION AND FOCUS

— Your practical pointer :

My eyes are **constantly** *fixed on the ball,*
before and whilst I'm hitting it.

My eyes are **constantly** *fixed on the ball,*
before and whilst I'm hitting it.

My eyes are **constantly** *fixed on the ball,*
before and whilst I'm hitting it.

NOW IT'S YOUR TURN
SET YOUR OWN GOALS RELATING TO
CONCENTRATION AND FOCUS :

MY GOALS	WHAT I WANT	WHY
Number 1		
Number 2		
Number 3		

Create your own affirmations and pointers below (always in the present tense). Find out what's right for you because this section is not complete without *your* input.

Concentration and Focus is directing all your attention, thoughts and energy towards the right thing at the right time. It is using your ability to apply yourself one hundred percent to whatever you are doing, whilst developing a relaxed detachment and calmness within yourself. During your match focus on the point at hand and take one point at a time. Trying to anticipate the score ahead of time will be distracting and unuseful. No match is ever won until the last point has been scored, so keep your emotions at bay until you have hit that last winner! Focusing on something between points and when changing ends will help avoid distractions. Everyone has something different, many players straighten the strings on their rackets, others focus on part of the net etc., find out what suits you.

Know that your subconscious mind works through association of ideas, so use it to your advantage. For example, one player found mentally repeating the word "Ball, Ball, Ball" when preparing to smash to be of great assistance and used it regularly in practice to help focus on and consistently smash the ball. When having to smash in matches, use of this "trigger word" assisted the player to block out all distractions, focus on the ball, leave the preparation and timing up to natural ability and successfully complete the shot. Everyone has something different, work out what may be useful for you. Similarly with set patterns or "rituals", for example, just before serving, perhaps you bounce the ball three times, breathe deeply, visualize where you want to place your serve and then toss the ball. Find areas where you can create your own rituals as these will assist you to be relaxed, focused and to turn on "your automatic". With association of ideas, something as simple as wearing your "winning socks" or favourite tennis shirt, help your subconscious mind reproduce the same feelings you experienced when you were succeeding or just feeling good. Whatever it is, use every element you can to help improve your performance level.

During play, thinking about concentrating or about your technique can actually end up destroying concentration (however, conscious attention is important in practice and whilst learning). For many players the most favourable state **whilst playing** is one where they think about absolutely nothing and totally disconnect, effectively they are on "automatic". In matches you slide in and out of this state and the next best thing to thinking about nothing, is focusing on just one thing, perhaps repeating your favourite affirmation or concentrating only on the ball. Everyone is an individual and different methods suit different people, find out which combinations suit you.

Now form affirmations for your goals and again use the following exercise to clear any negative thoughts, if needed.

NEGATIVE CLEARING EXERCISE

Write each negative thought down as it occurs to you, on a blank piece of paper, **which you can rip up and throw away later.** Think about them for a while and work out which ones have the most power over you. Counteract each one by writing your own positive affirmation(s) or by using an affirmation from the preceding section.

Repeat this process, clearing and releasing each destructive thought as and when it arises, replacing it with something positive. Then feel and visualize yourself as vividly as possible in the context of your new affirmation.

Affirmations when **used on a regular basis** will become second nature to you and automatic in your reactions, they will assist you to remain centred, calm and determined in your progress towards your goals. Knowing how your subconscious mind works will assist you to break through the barriers and limitations you have imposed on yourself, enroll its help and use it! You are the only person who can "stand guard" over your conscious thoughts and the more you are aware of these, the more you can be in charge of your future and the results of your tennis matches!

Remember **YOU ARE A WINNER !**

YOUR COMPLETE CHECK LIST

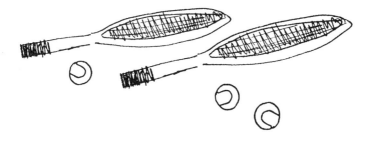

1. SELF-MOTIVATION

1

I have the ability to win this match …
I believe in myself.

2

I have the strength, power and energy to win.

3

I have the determination and resiliance to achieve my goals.

4

After each winning point, I show a positive physical reaction.

2. SELF-CONFIDENCE

1

I know I can win ... I believe in myself.

2

I have strength and stamina ... the power is within me.

3

I have the mental and physical ability to win this match.

4

I NEVER show my opponent what I'm thinking or feeling when I'm unhappy.

3. SELF-DISCIPLINE

1

I remain calm and relaxed all match ... I believe in myself.

2

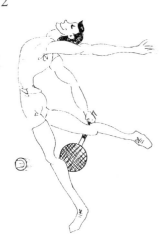

I always play to the best of my ability.

3

I act clearly and decisively ... I let nothing upset me.

4

I preserve my physical energy ... as much as possible.

4. SELF-ESTEEM

1

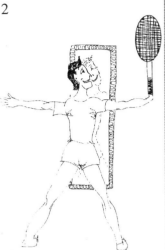

Whatever the outcome, I am kind to myself ... I believe in myself.

2

I praise and encourage myself when I play well.

3

I forgive myself if I make a mistake ... I forget it and get on with the game.

4

I keep my posture straight and my head UP at all times.

5. SELF-IMPROVEMENT

1

I always keep my goals in sight ...
I believe in myself.

2

I have the wisdom and patience necessary to achieve all my desires.

3

I recognize my progress and I continue onwards and upwards.

4

I breathe DEEPLY and exhale slowly between every point.

6. CONCENTRATION AND FOCUS

1

I remain lucid ... I give my complete attention during each point.

2

I have the ability to concentrate and focus all my energies.

3

I forget all other points and focus on the one at hand.

4

My eyes are **constantly** fixed on the ball, before and whilst I'm hitting it.

POWER LIST

Write below the affirmations you feel most at ease with or the ones which are the most important for you. Refer to this list at regular intervals and just before playing matches.

SELF-MOTIVATION

SELF-CONFIDENCE

SELF-DISCIPLINE

SELF-ESTEEM

SELF-IMPROVEMENT

CONCENTRATION AND FOCUS

Life is a game, play it!

Tennis is a game, know it

and above all, enjoy it!

GAME,
SET
AND
MATCH

READING LIST:

The Power of Your Subconscious Mind
Dr. Joseph Murphy, D.R.S.,Ph.D.,D.D.,LL.D.   Simon & Schuster

The Will to Win!
Paula Whittam   Sapphire Publishing

Tennis, the Mind Game
Marlin M. McKenzie, Ed. D.   Dell Publishing

Mental Toughness Training for Sports
James E. Loehr, Ed. D.   Plume (Penguin Group)

The Inner Game of Tennis
W. Timothy Gallwey   Bantam

Body, Mind and Sport
John Douillard   Bantam

The Warrier Athlete
Dan Millman   Stillpoint Publishing

Unlimited Power
Anthony Robbins   Simon & Schuster

Creative Visualization
Shakti Gawain   New World Library

Meditation for Everybody
Louis Proto   Penguin